MARY BERRY

Favourite Cakes

MARY BERRY

Favourite Cakes

Photography by Philip Wilkins

WEIDENFELD & NICOLSON

Mary Berry

Mary Berry is one of Britain's foremost cookery writers and broadcasters. She has written 28 cookery books, including a *Quick and Easy Cake Book* and the comprehensive *Mary Berry's Complete Cookbook*, and frequently appears on television. She made seven series for Thames TV, shown on *Good Afternoon* and *Afternoon Plus*. The BBC-TV series *Mary Berry's Ultimate Cakes* was accompanied by a best-selling book of the same name and was followed by *Mary Berry at Home*. She also, with Arthur Negus, co-presented three programmes on Georgian and Victorian food.

Mary Berry lives in Buckinghamshire, where she runs Aga workshops in her beautiful kitchen; 6,000 Aga owners have attended.

Contents

THE BASICS

Use the finest ingredients,
measure them carefully
and follow these simple
instructions and you will have
success every time.

Introduction

I have always enjoyed making cakes for family and friends; for this book I have selected some of my most popular cakes for a variety of occasions.

For special celebrations there is a chocolate cake and a coffee almond cake, as well as a lime meringue roulade which doubles as a dessert. Freshly baked, crisp orange fork biscuits and lemon shortbread could accompany creamy mousses or fools; they certainly won't stay long in the biscuit tin. Wholesome apricot and sunflower flapjacks are good for lunch boxes. Rich fruited tea loaf and spiced ginger cake both freeze well; for best results, freeze the ginger cake un-iced.

I have also used some ingredients that are new in the shops. Dried sour cherries can be found alongside the dried fruits in large supermarkets and are a delicious addition to muffins. Tropical fruits are now readily available in a dried, moist, ready-to-eat form. Choose from pineapple, papaya, mango, pear, peach and others to make a delicious light tropical fruit cake. This little book wouldn't be complete without a Victoria sandwich cake and a traybake: the mincemeat version I have chosen is a top favourite and keeps well.

Special chocolate cake

MAKES A 20 CM/8 INCH CAKE

50 g/2 oz cocoa, sifted
5 tablespoons boiling water
3 eggs
150 g/5 oz low-fat natural yogurt
125 g/4 oz soft baking margarine
275 g/10 oz caster sugar
175 g/6 oz self-raising flour
1 rounded teaspoon baking
    powder

White chocolate ganache

300 g/11 oz white chocolate,
    chopped
300 ml/½ pint double cream

To decorate

about 125 g/4 oz dark chocolate

Preheat the oven to 180°C/350°F/Gas Mark 4. Lightly grease two 20 cm/8 inch sandwich tins and line the bases with greased greaseproof paper.

Sift the cocoa into a large mixing bowl, add the water and blend until smooth. Leave to cool slightly. Add the eggs, yogurt, margarine and sugar, sift in the flour and baking powder and beat well until smooth. Divide the mixture between the two tins and level the surface. Bake in the oven for 25–30 minutes, until the cakes are well risen, firm to the touch and just beginning to shrink away from the sides of the tins. Leave to cool in the tins for a few minutes, then turn out, peel off the lining paper and leave to cool completely on a wire rack.

To decorate the cake, make chocolate caraque or curls. For caraque, as shown, melt the dark chocolate (page 36) and pour a thin layer on to a smooth, scratch-proof surface. Spread the chocolate thinly using a palette knife and leave until nearly set. Hold a long, sharp, flexible knife at an angle and shave the chocolate off the surface. For chocolate curls, use a swivel peeler along the flat side of a chocolate bar at room temperature. Chocolate-flavoured cake covering is particularly good for this.

For the white chocolate ganache, put the chocolate in a heatproof bowl. Bring the cream to the boil, pour over the chocolate and leave to stand, without stirring, for about 5 minutes, then stir until smooth. Leave to cool. Whisk the cooled mixture until it has the consistency of thickly whipped cream.

When completely cold, sandwich the cakes with half the ganache and spread the rest over the sides and top of the cake. Decorate with the chocolate caraque or curls.

LIME MERINGUE ROULADE

SERVES 8–10

5 egg whites
275 g/10 oz caster sugar
50 g/2 oz flaked almonds

Lime filling
grated zest and juice of
   2 large limes
40 g/1½ oz cornflour
2 egg yolks
85 g/3 oz caster sugar
3 tablespoons double cream

Preheat the oven to 220°C/425°F/Gas Mark 7. Line a 33 x 23 cm/13 x 9 inch Swiss roll tin with greased nonstick baking paper.

First make the filling: put the grated lime zest and juice in a small bowl, add the cornflour and blend well. Bring 300 ml/½ pint water to the boil in a saucepan and stir into the cornflour mixture. Return the mixture to the pan and simmer gently, stirring constantly until it forms a thick custard. Mix the egg yolks and sugar together and stir into the lime mixture. Bring back to the boil, stirring until just bubbling. Remove from the heat and leave to cool, stirring occasionally.

For the roulade, whisk the egg whites in an electric mixer on full speed until very stiff. With the mixer still on high speed, gradually add the sugar, a teaspoon at a time, whisking well between each addition. Whisk until very stiff and all the sugar has been added. Spread the meringue mixture into the prepared tin and sprinkle with the almonds. Place the tin fairly near the top of the oven and bake for about 8–10 minutes, until very golden. Then lower the temperature to 160°C/325°F/Gas Mark 3 and bake the roulade for a further 15 minutes, until firm to the touch.

Turn the meringue on to a sheet of nonstick baking paper, almond side down. Peel off the paper from the base of the meringue and leave to cool for about 10 minutes.

Lightly whip the cream and fold into the cooled lime custard. Spread evenly over the meringue. Roll up the meringue fairly tightly from one of the long sides to form a roulade. Wrap in nonstick baking paper and chill well before serving.

COFFEE ALMOND CAKE

MAKES A 20 CM/8 INCH CAKE

3 eggs
125 g/4 oz caster sugar
85 g/3 oz self-raising flour

Coffee buttercream icing
325 g/12 oz icing sugar, sifted
200 g/7 oz butter, softened
2 teaspoons instant coffee
   dissolved in 2 tablespoons
   hot water

To decorate
175 g/6 oz flaked almonds,
   toasted (page 36)

Preheat the oven to 190°C/375°F/Gas Mark 5. Lightly grease a 20 cm/8 inch deep round cake tin and line the base with greased greaseproof paper.

Put the eggs and caster sugar into a large bowl and whisk at full speed with an electric whisk until the mixture is pale and thick enough to just leave a trail when the whisk is lifted from the bowl. Sift the flour over the surface of the mixture and gently fold in using a metal spoon or spatula. Turn into the prepared cake tin, tilting the tin to level the surface. Bake in the oven for about 30 minutes, until well risen and golden brown. Turn out, peel off the lining paper and leave to cool on a wire rack.

For the icing: put the sugar, butter and coffee into a bowl and beat until smooth. Cut the cake in half horizontally and use about two-thirds of the icing to fill and cover the cake. Press the toasted flaked almonds all over the top and sides of the cake. Put the remaining buttercream icing into a piping bag and pipe rosettes on to the cake.

Fatless whisked sponges do not keep, so either freeze, or eat on the day it is made.

LIGHT TROPICAL FRUIT CAKE

MAKES AN 18 CM/7 INCH CAKE

125 g/4 oz soft baking margarine
125 g/4 oz caster sugar
2 eggs, beaten
175 g/6 oz self-raising flour
1 teaspoon baking powder
1 tablespoon milk
225 g/8 oz mixed ready-to-eat
  dried fruits, such as mango,
  papaya, pear, pineapple,
  chopped

To decorate
85 g/3 oz icing sugar, sifted
about 5 teaspoons boiling water
50 g/2 oz mixed dried fruits (as
  above), chopped

Preheat the oven to 180°C/350°F/Gas Mark 4. Lightly grease an 18 cm/7 inch deep round cake tin and line the base with greased greaseproof paper.

Put the margarine, caster sugar, eggs, flour, baking powder and milk into a mixing bowl and beat well for about 2 minutes, until evenly blended. Fold in the chopped fruit, then spoon the mixture into the prepared cake tin and level the surface. Bake in the oven for about 1 hour, until golden and firm to the touch. Leave to cool in the tin for about 10 minutes, then turn out, peel off the lining paper and leave to cool completely on a wire rack.

To decorate, mix the icing sugar with the water until smooth. Drizzle over the top of the cake and scatter over the chopped dried fruits.

VICTORIA SANDWICH CAKE

MAKES A 20 CM/8 INCH CAKE

225 g/8 oz soft baking
   margarine
225 g/8 oz caster sugar
4 eggs
225 g/8 oz self-raising flour
2 teaspoons baking powder

To finish
about 4 tablespoons raspberry
   or strawberry jam
150 ml/¼ pint double cream,
   whipped, or Vanilla
   Buttercream (page 37)
caster sugar to sprinkle

Preheat the oven to 180°C/350°F/Gas Mark 4. Lightly grease two 20 cm/8 inch sandwich tins and line the bases with greased greaseproof paper.

Put the margarine, sugar, eggs, flour and baking powder into a large bowl and beat well until thoroughly blended. Divide the mixture between the prepared cake tins and level the surfaces. Bake in the oven for about 25 minutes, until well risen and the tops of the cakes spring back when lightly pressed with a finger. Leave to cool in the tins for a few moments, then turn out, peel off the lining paper and leave to cool completely on a wire rack.

When completely cold, sandwich the cakes together with the jam and whipped cream or buttercream and sprinkle with caster sugar.

Spiced ginger cake

MAKES 9 PIECES

125 g/4 oz soft baking margarine
85 g/3 oz caster sugar
125 g/4 oz black treacle
150 g/5 oz self-raising flour
1 teaspoon baking powder
1 teaspoon ground ginger
2 eggs
2 tablespoons milk

Icing
125 g/4 oz icing sugar
2 tablespoons stem ginger syrup
1 cm/½ inch piece of stem
  ginger, thinly shredded

Preheat the oven to 180°C/350°F/Gas Mark 4. Lightly grease an 18 cm/7 inch square shallow cake tin and line the base with greased greaseproof paper.

Put all the cake ingredients into a large bowl and beat well for about 2 minutes, until well blended. Turn the mixture into the prepared tin and level the top. Bake in the oven for about 30−35 minutes, until the cake has shrunk from the sides of the tin and springs back when pressed lightly with the fingertips. Leave to cool in the tin for a few minutes, then turn out, peel off the lining paper and leave to cool completely on a wire rack.

For the icing, sift the icing sugar into a bowl and add the stem ginger syrup and 2−3 teaspoons water. Mix until smooth, then stir in the shredded stem ginger. Pour the icing over the cake and leave to set. To serve, cut into 9 squares.

Sour cherry muffins

MAKES 12 MUFFINS

275 g/10 oz plain flour
3 teaspoons baking powder
2 eggs
85 g/3 oz caster sugar
250 ml/8 fl oz milk
125 g/4 oz butter, melted
   and cooled
few drops of vanilla essence
175 g/6 oz dried sour cherries,*
   roughly chopped
nibbed sugar, preserving sugar
   or crushed sugar cubes

*Available from large super-
markets and health food shops.
Substitute dried cranberries or
dried blueberries if you wish.

Preheat the oven to 200°C/400°F/Gas Mark 6.
Lightly grease a 12-hole muffin tray, or line with paper
muffin cases.

Sift the flour and baking powder into a bowl. Put the
eggs, caster sugar, milk, melted butter and vanilla essence
into a separate large bowl and stir until well mixed.
Quickly stir the flour and baking powder into the egg
mixture, mixing only until the ingredients have just
come together and no longer, so as not to knock out
too much air. Carefully fold in the cherries. Divide
the mixture between the muffin cases and sprinkle with
nibbed sugar. Bake in the oven for about 30 minutes or
until well risen, firm and golden. Serve warm.

MINCEMEAT TRAYBAKE

MAKES 18 SQUARES

225 g/8 oz soft baking margarine
225 g/8 oz caster sugar
275 g/10 oz self-raising flour
2 teaspoons baking powder
4 eggs
1 tablespoon milk
225 g/8 oz mincemeat
125 g/4 oz currants

Preheat the oven to 180°C/350°F/Gas Mark 4. Lightly grease a 30 x 23 cm/12 x 9 inch shallow tin (about 4 cm/1½ inches deep) and line the base with greased greaseproof paper.

Put the margarine, sugar, flour, baking powder, eggs and milk into a large mixing bowl and beat well for about 2 minutes, until well blended. Gently mix in the mincemeat and currants. Turn the mixture into the prepared tin and level the top. Bake in the oven for about 40−45 minutes, until the cake has shrunk from the sides of the tin and springs back when lightly pressed with a finger. Leave to cool in the tin. To serve, cut into 18 squares.

ORANGE FORK BISCUITS

MAKES ABOUT 30 BISCUITS

225 g/8 oz butter, softened
125 g/4 oz caster sugar
grated zest of 2 small oranges
275 g/10 oz self-raising flour

Preheat the oven to 180°C/350°F/Gas Mark 4. Lightly grease three baking sheets.

Put the butter, sugar and grated orange zest into a mixing bowl and cream together until soft. Sift in the flour and work to a stiff paste, using your hands to bring the mixture together. Divide the mixture into walnut-sized pieces and place on the baking sheets, leaving room for the biscuits to spread. Press the biscuits with a fork to flatten them, then bake in the oven for about 15–20 minutes, until pale golden. Lift the biscuits off the baking tray with a palette knife or fish slice and leave to cool completely on a wire rack.

RICH FRUITED TEA LOAF

MAKES TWO 450 G/1 LB LOAVES

175 g/6 oz currants
175 g/6 oz sultanas
175 g/6 oz light
    muscovado sugar
300 ml/½ pint strong hot tea
275 g/10 oz self-raising
    flour, sifted
1 egg, beaten
2 tablespoons fine-cut
    marmalade

Start making this tea loaf the night before you want to bake it. Put the currants, sultanas and sugar into a bowl, pour over the hot tea, cover and leave overnight.

Preheat the oven to 150°C/300°F/Gas Mark 2. Lightly grease two 450 g/1 lb loaf tins and line the bases with greased greaseproof paper (it is best cooked in two smaller tins, rather than one 900 g/2 lb tin).

Stir the flour, egg and marmalade into the fruit mixture, mix thoroughly, then turn into the prepared tins and level the surface. Bake in the oven for about 1–1¼ hours, until well risen and firm to the touch; a fine skewer inserted into the centre should come out clean. Leave to cool in the tins for about 10 minutes, then turn out and leave to cool completely on a wire rack. Serve sliced and buttered.

LEMON SHORTBREAD

MAKES ABOUT 18–20 PIECES

175 g/6 oz butter, softened
85 g/3 oz caster sugar
175 g/6 oz plain flour, sifted
85 g/3 oz ground rice*
grated zest of 2 lemons
caster sugar to sprinkle

*Ground rice gives a good short texture to the shortbread. If you like a more crunchy shortbread, replace the ground rice with semolina.

Preheat the oven to 160°C/325°F/Gas Mark 3. Lightly grease a 30 x 23 cm/12 x 9 inch shallow tin (about 4 cm/1½ inches deep).

Put the butter and sugar into a mixing bowl and cream together with a wooden spoon until light and fluffy. Work in the flour, ground rice and lemon zest and knead well until smooth. Press the mixture into the prepared tin and level the surface. Bake in the oven for about 35 minutes, until pale golden brown.

Mark the shortbread into fingers or wedges and leave in the tin until quite cold. Using a palette knife, lift out on to a wire rack and sprinkle with caster sugar.

APRICOT AND SUNFLOWER FLAPJACKS

MAKES 8 BARS

125 g/4 oz margarine
125 g/4 oz demerara sugar
1 tablespoon golden syrup
175 g/6 oz rolled oats
50 g/2 oz no-soak apricots,
   snipped into pieces
50 g/2 oz sunflower seeds

Preheat the oven to 160°C/325°F/Gas Mark 3. Lightly grease an 18 cm/7 inch square shallow cake tin.

Put the margarine, sugar and golden syrup in a saucepan and melt over a low heat. Stir in the oats, apricots and sunflower seeds and mix well. Turn into the prepared tin and level the surface. Bake in the oven for about 35 minutes, until golden brown.

Leave to cool in the tin for 10 minutes. Mark into 8 bars and leave to cool until they are firm enough to lift out of the tin with a palette knife. Transfer to a wire rack and leave to cool completely.

The Basics

Baking know-how

All-in-one method

The all-in-one method means just that. All of the main ingredients go into the bowl to be mixed at the same time, making this a quick and foolproof way of producing some of the best cakes. Soft baking margarine must be used (see below) and baking powder is needed as well as self-raising flour, to compensate for the air not being incorporated during the initial creaming stages.

Soft baking margarine

This should be used for the all-in-one method of cake making as it needs to be mixed with the other cake ingredients straight from the refrigerator. Hard margarines are simply too difficult to mix for this quick method. Low-fat margarines cannot be used as their high water content makes them unsuitable for baking. You can use butter, but it must first be softened to a creamy consistency.

Eggs

Use large eggs for these cake recipes. Eggs are generally sold in three sizes: extra large, large and medium. Eggs can be used straight from the refrigerator, but when whisking egg whites, for example for meringues, you will obtain a larger volume if the whites have been brought to room temperature.

SUGARS

Caster sugar is best for most cake recipes as it is easy to incorporate into the mixture. If granulated sugar is used the cake is likely to have a speckled top, as the sugar will not fully dissolve during baking. If liked, light muscovado sugar can be substituted for caster sugar in cakes.

For brown meringues, use half caster and half light muscovado sugar.

OVEN TEMPERATURES

Regrettably, no two ovens are the same, whether they are gas, electric or fan assisted. The baking times I have given have been tested many times, but it is always worth checking a cake a little before the specified time, just in case your oven is slightly hotter, for instance. Then, make a note by the side of the recipe so that you have a reference for next time.

TESTING CAKES

Each baked recipe gives a test for doneness, for example if the cake is firm and springy to the touch, or the mixture is shrinking away from the sides of the tin. Use these as well as the baking time guidelines to make sure your cakes are perfectly cooked.

STORING AND FREEZING

Light fruit cakes are always best eaten soon after making. Alternatively they can be securely wrapped and frozen. Freeze either whole, or in pieces, well wrapped in foil, cling film or strong polythene bags, for up to 3 months. Do not store cakes and biscuits in the same tin, as the moisture from the cake will make the biscuits go soggy.

TOASTED ALMONDS

Flaked almonds can be bought ready toasted, but these are quite expensive. Toast the flaked almonds yourself by placing them in a thin layer on a baking sheet. Brown under a hot grill, watching them carefully and turning them often to obtain an even colour and to prevent burning. Slivered and chopped nib almonds can be toasted in the same way

MELTING CHOCOLATE

Chocolate does not need a high heat to melt; remember how easily a bar of chocolate melts on a sunny windowsill or in a child's pocket! Break the chocolate into squares or chop into a bowl and set the bowl over a saucepan of hot water. Stir from time to time until smooth. Be careful not to get a drop of water into the bowl, otherwise the chocolate will become irretrievably sticky and lumpy. Alternatively, melt in a microwave oven.

VANILLA BUTTERCREAM

125 g/4 oz butter, softened
225 g/8 oz icing sugar, sifted
2–3 drops of vanilla essence

Put the butter in a bowl and beat until light. Gradually beat in the icing sugar and vanilla essence until pale and creamy.

Classic Cooking

STARTERS

Lesley Waters A former chef and now a popular television cook, appearing regularly on *Ready Steady Cook* and *Can't Cook Won't Cook.* Author of several cookery books.

VEGETABLE SOUPS

Elisabeth Luard Cookery writer for the *Sunday Telegraph Magazine* and author of *European Peasant Food* and *European Festival Food*, which won a Glenfiddich Award.

GOURMET SALADS

Sonia Stevenson The first woman chef in the UK to be awarded a Michelin star, at the Horn of Plenty in Devon. Author of *The Magic of Saucery* and *Fresh Ways with Fish.*

FISH AND SHELLFISH

Gordon Ramsay Chef/proprietor of London's Aubergine restaurant, recently awarded its second Michelin star, and author of *A Passion for Flavour.*

CHICKEN, DUCK AND GAME

Nick Nairn Chef/patron of Braeval restaurant near Aberfoyle in Scotland, whose BBC-TV series *Wild Harvest* was last summer's most successful cookery series, accompanied by a book.

LIVERS, SWEETBREADS AND KIDNEYS

Simon Hopkinson Former chef/patron at London's Bibendum restaurant, columnist and author of *Roast Chicken and Other Stories* and *The Prawn Cocktail Years.*

VEGETARIAN

Rosamond Richardson Author of several vegetarian titles, including *The Great Green Cookbook* and *Food from Green Places.*

PASTA

Joy Davies One of the creators of *BBC Good Food Magazine*, she has been food editor of *She, Woman* and *Options* and written for the *Guardian, Daily Telegraph* and *Harpers & Queen.*

CHEESE DISHES

Rose Elliot The UK's most successful vegetarian cookery writer and author of many books, including *Not Just a Load of Old Lentils* and *The Classic Vegetarian Cookbook.*

POTATO DISHES

Patrick McDonald Former chef/patron of the acclaimed Epicurean restaurant in Cheltenham, and food consultant to Sir Rocco Forte Hotels.

BISTRO

Anne Willan Founder and director of La Varenne Cookery School in Burgundy and West Virginia. Author of many books and a specialist in French cuisine.

ITALIAN

Anna Del Conte Author of several books on Italian food, including *The Gastronomy of Italy, Secrets from an Italian Kitchen* and *The Classic Food of Northern Italy* (chosen as the 1996 Guild of Food Writers Book of the Year).

VIETNAMESE

Nicole Routhier One of the United States' most popular cookery writers, her books include *Cooking Under Wraps, Nicole Routhier's Fruit Cookbook* and the award-winning *The Foods of Vietnam.*

MALAYSIAN

Jill Dupleix One of Australia's best known cookery writers and broadcasters, with columns in the *Sydney Morning Herald* and *Elle.* Her books include *New Food* and *Allegro al dente.*

PEKING CUISINE

Helen Chen Author of *Chinese Home Cooking,* she learned to cook traditional Peking dishes from her mother, Joyce Chen, the *grande dame* of Chinese cooking in the United States.

STIR-FRIES

Kay Fairfax A writer and broadcaster whose books include *100 Great Stir-fries, Homemade* and *The Australian Christmas Book.*

NOODLES

Terry Durack Australia's most widely read restaurant critic and co-editor of the *Sydney Morning Herald Good Food Guide.* He is the author of *YUM,* a book of stories and recipes.

NORTH INDIAN CURRIES

Pat Chapman Founded the Curry Club in 1982. A regular broadcaster on television and radio, he is the author of 20 books, which have sold more than 1 million copies.

GRILLS AND BARBECUES

Brian Turner Chef/patron of Turner's in Knightsbridge and one of Britain's most popular food broadcasters; he appears frequently on *Ready Steady Cook, Food and Drink* and many other television programmes.

SUMMER AND WINTER CASSEROLES

Anton Edelmann Maître Chef des Cuisines at the Savoy Hotel, London. Author of six cookery books, he has also appeared on television.

TRADITIONAL PUDDINGS

Tessa Bramley Chef/patron of the acclaimed Old Vicarage restaurant in Ridgeway, Derbyshire and author of *The Instinctive Cook.*

DECORATED CAKES

Jane Asher Author of several cookery books and a novel. She has also appeared in her own television series, *Jane Asher's Christmas* (1995).

FAVOURITE CAKES

Mary Berry One of Britain's leading cookery writers, her numerous books include *Mary Berry's Ultimate Cake Book.* She has made many television and radio appearances.

ICE CREAMS AND SEMI FREDDI

Ann and Franco Taruschio Owners of the renowned Walnut Tree Inn near Abergavenny in Wales, soon to appear in a television series, *Franco and Friends: Food from the Walnut Tree.* They have written three books together.

Photographs © Philip Wilkins 1997

First published in 1997 by
George Weidenfeld & Nicolson
The Orion Publishing Group
Orion House
5 Upper St Martin's Lane
London WC2H 9EA

British Library Cataloguing-in-Publication data
A catalogue record for this book is available from
the British Library

ISBN 0 297 82340 X

Designed by Lucy Holmes
Edited by Maggie Ramsay
Food styling by Louise Pickford
Typesetting by Tiger Typeset